T0002302

GROWING PEACE

A STORY OF FARMING, MUSIC, AND RELIGIOUS HARMONY

RICHARD SOBOL

LEE & LOW BOOKS INC. ◆ NEW YORK

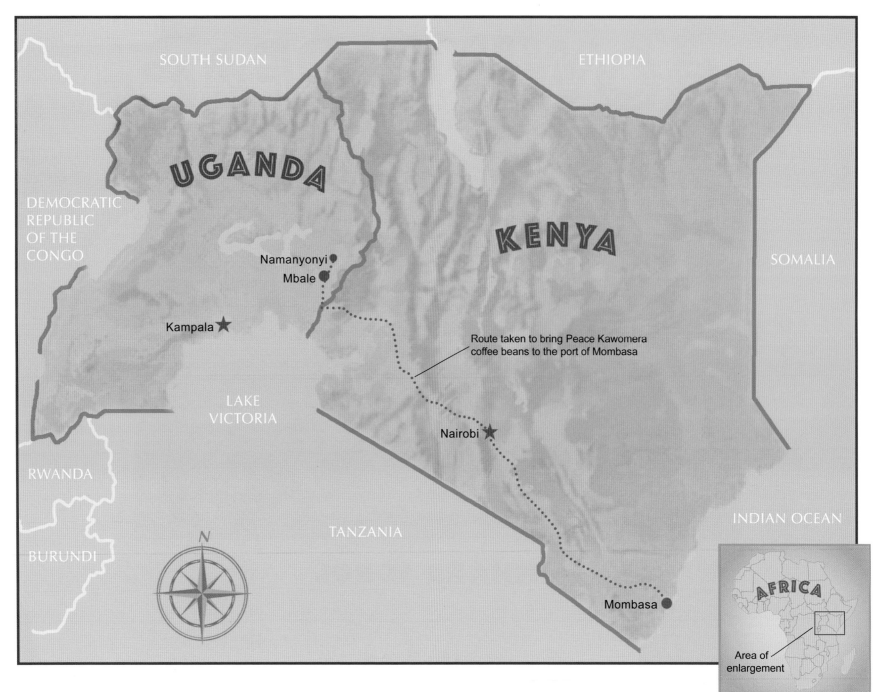

SOUTH SUDAN

ETHIOPIA

UGANDA

DEMOCRATIC
REPUBLIC
OF THE
CONGO

KENYA

SOMALIA

Namanyonyi

Mbale

Kampala ★

Route taken to bring Peace Kawomera
coffee beans to the port of Mombasa

LAKE
VICTORIA

Nairobi ★

RWANDA

INDIAN OCEAN

TANZANIA

BURUNDI

N

Mombasa

AFRICA

Area of
enlargement

Children playing a game of futbol on a hillside outside of Namanyonyi

As the sun sets in eastern Uganda, the blazing heat fades and a cool wind settles in the valley. In the small, dusty village of Namanyonyi, near the city of Mbale, people enjoy the fresh evening air. Some children play soccer, which they call *futbol*. Others sing songs and tap out rhythms on plastic water jugs and homemade wooden drums.

Planting seeds in a vegetable garden as a rainstorm moves in

While the children play and sing in the fading light, their parents finish working in their fields and small gardens nearby. They harvest sweet potatoes, corn, beans, and coffee. The vegetables go straight to their dinner tables, but not the coffee. Ugandans prefer to drink tea. The coffee is the one crop the villagers sell to other countries around the world.

At the top of a rounded hill alongside a rocky dirt path stands a hand-painted sign that reads: PEACE KAWOMERA (Delicious Peace) GROWERS CO-OP SOCIETY LTD. On one side are symbols representing three religions: a cross for Christianity, a six-pointed Star of David for Judaism, and a five-pointed star and crescent for Islam.

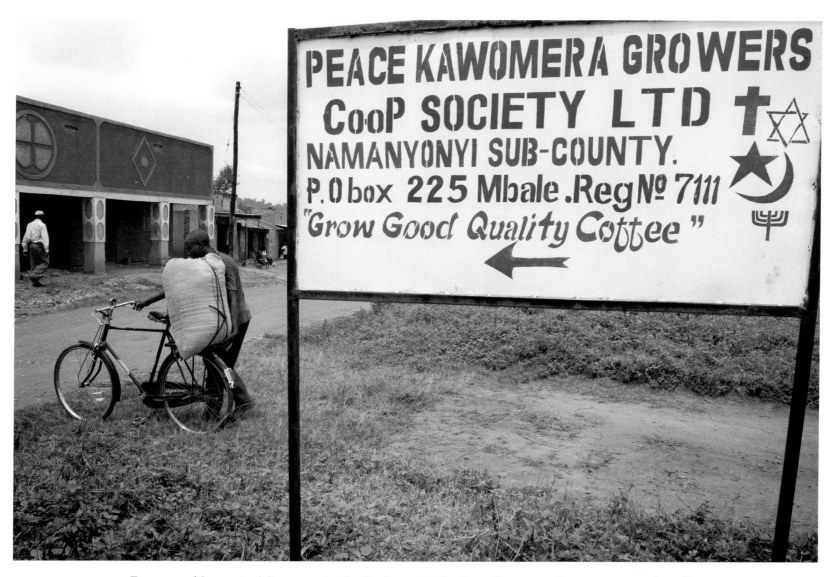

Farmer on his way to deliver a sack of coffee beans to the Peace Kawomera Growers cooperative office

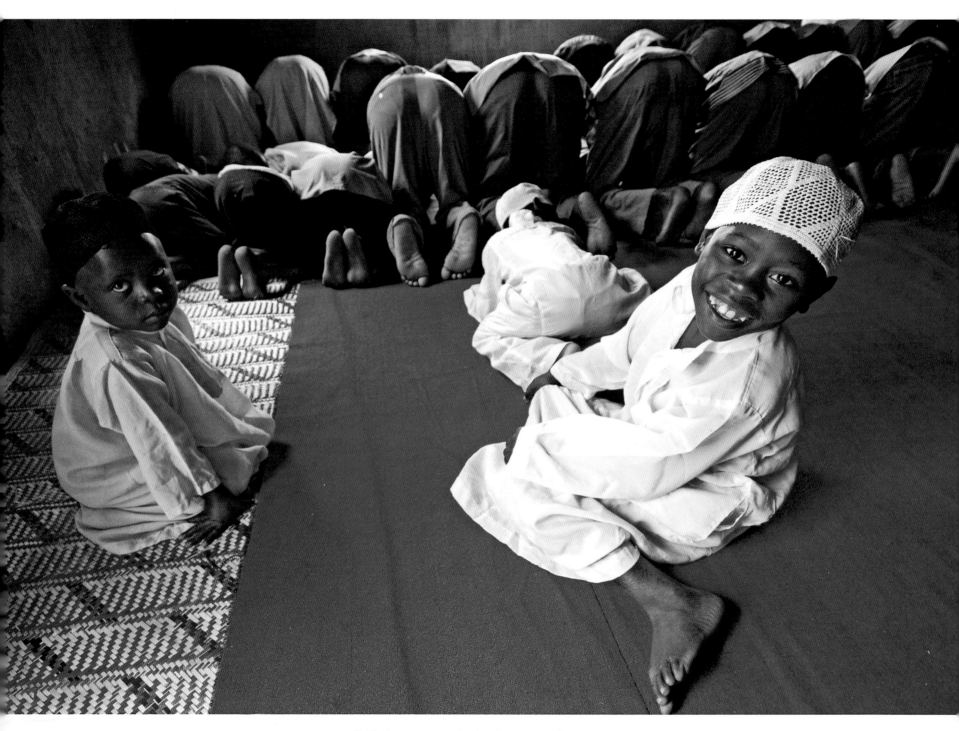

Friday prayers at Nankusi Mosque of Namanyonyi

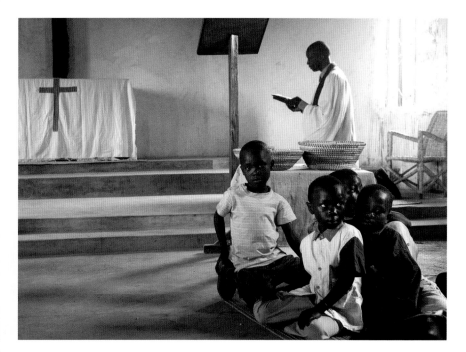

Leader reading Sunday prayers at
Namanyonyi Anglican Church

Saturday morning Sabbath prayers at
Namanyonyi Synagogue

Christianity, Judaism, and Islam are the religions of the villagers; and the farmers have joined together to create an interfaith farming cooperative. In some places in the world, people fight and even go to war because they have different religious beliefs. But in the village of Namanyonyi, neighbors of different religions help one another and work together to make life better for all.

What happened in Namanyonyi that made people want to live in harmony and try to improve their lives as a peaceful community?

The answer begins more than one hundred years ago, at the start of the twentieth century. As a young man, Semei Kakungulu, a Ugandan tribal leader, had been converted to Christianity by a missionary. But after studying the Bible on his own for many years, Kakungulu was drawn to follow the religious laws and teachings found in the first five books of the Bible, known to Jews as the Torah. Many of Kakungulu's people also began to observe these laws and teachings. The group became known as the Abayudaya, which means "Jewish people" or "people of Judah" in Luganda, the local language.

Not everyone joined Kakungulu. Others, even some members of his own family, maintained their beliefs in the religious laws and teachings of Christianity, or of Islam, which had been introduced to the region by the mid-nineteenth century.

Semei Kakungulu (1869–1928), founder of the Abayudaya

Women carrying water jugs and food for dairy cows passing by Moses Synagogue

In the 1970s and 1980s, a series of civil wars was fought in Uganda. People of all religions faced persecution as two brutal leaders battled for power and control. The country and its people suffered great hardships during this long time of war.

As Uganda grew more peaceful in the 1990s, two students from the United States came to explore the rural countryside. They were surprised to discover six small Jewish synagogues near Mbale. While there, the students made recordings of the Abayudaya singing ancient Hebrew prayers set to new African melodies and rhythms that they had written themselves. Some of the music became popular in the United States and was played on the radio.

One of the leaders of the Abayudaya, J. J. (Joab Jonadav) Keki, is a talented musician as well as a coffee farmer. He wrote many of the new melodies that were on the recordings. In 2001, J.J. was invited to be a guest music teacher at a children's summer camp in western Massachusetts.

When the camp season was over, J.J. wanted to explore as much of the United States as he could. Near Boston he saw the ocean for the first time and let out a shout when he touched the icy-cold waters of the Atlantic. He had his first tastes of pizza and ice cream, and they became his new favorite foods.

J. J. Keki pruning his coffee plants

J.J. walking along an Atlantic Ocean beach near Boston, Massachusetts

On Monday, September 10, J.J. took a train to New York City to meet a friend and tour the sights of Manhattan. They planned to start early the next morning with a visit to the World Trade Center.

On Tuesday morning, September 11, as a plane that was aimed at the World Trade Center Twin Towers roared low in the sky, J.J. was just coming out from a subway station. He looked up to see a plane hit one of the tall buildings. J.J.'s worried friend was later relieved to see a TV news report that showed J.J. running away from the dust and rubble of the collapsing towers. J.J. was safe, but quite shaken and shocked by the terrible event he had witnessed.

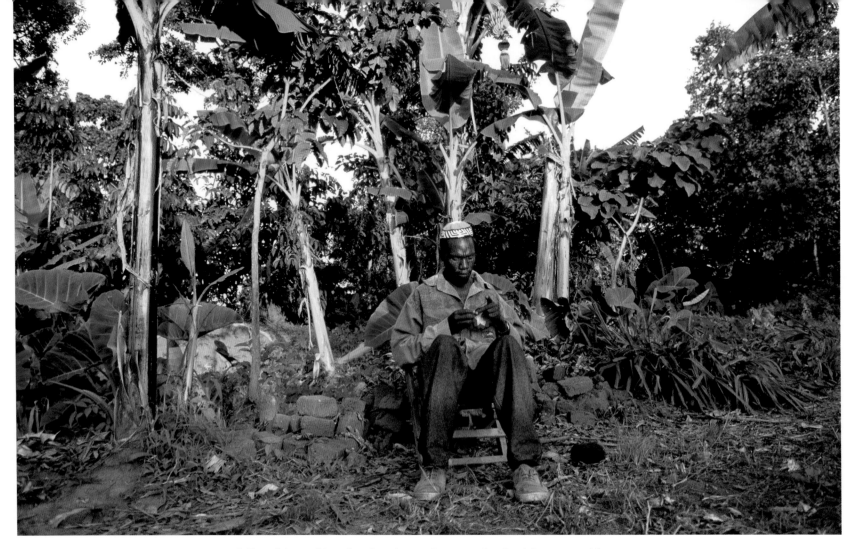

J.J. making a *kippah*, a head covering worn by Jewish men and boys

In November, J.J. flew home to Uganda and returned to Namanyonyi. He went back to farming his coffee and writing songs to sing and play on his guitar. But the memories of that September morning stayed with him. In J.J.'s mind, the terrorist attack had been carried out by people who did not want to accept religious differences. "Why should we be enemies because of our religions?" J.J. asked. He began to wonder what he could do to help bring people of different religions together instead.

J.J.'s home is full of children. Throughout the house and in the backyard, a steady stream of girls and boys move about. They run and chase one another, dodging between the scruffy chickens that call the yard their home. J.J. and his wife, Deborah, have eight children of their own, and they have adopted several others. Although J.J. is Jewish, some of the adopted children in his family are Christian and some are Muslim. The Muslim children worship at their mosque every Friday. That is a special day of prayer for Muslims. The Jewish children worship at their synagogue each Saturday. That is the Sabbath, the day of the week set aside for prayer and rest. For the Christian children, Sunday is the Sabbath, and they go to their church on that day to worship.

Wherever J.J. goes, children follow him and stay close by his side

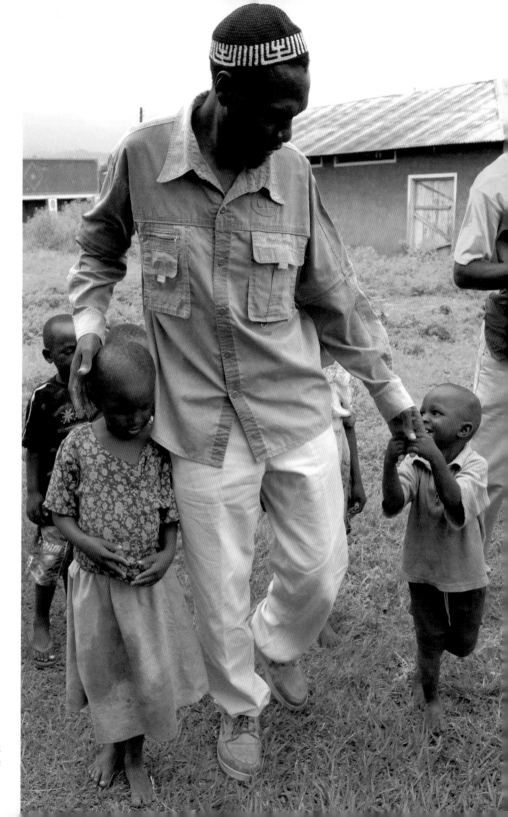

At night, some of J.J.'s children can be seen reading and studying near the soft yellow light of a kerosene lamp in his living room. The children help one another with homework as they write slowly and neatly in their thin, paperback notebooks.

Sitting on a small bench behind his home and surrounded by coffee plants, J.J. often tells his story. The children stare wide-eyed as J.J. explains that in 2001 he was nearly a victim of the terrorist attack in New York City. And then he tells them how that experience made him think about what he could do to help people live together in peace.

Children studying at night by the light of a kerosene lamp

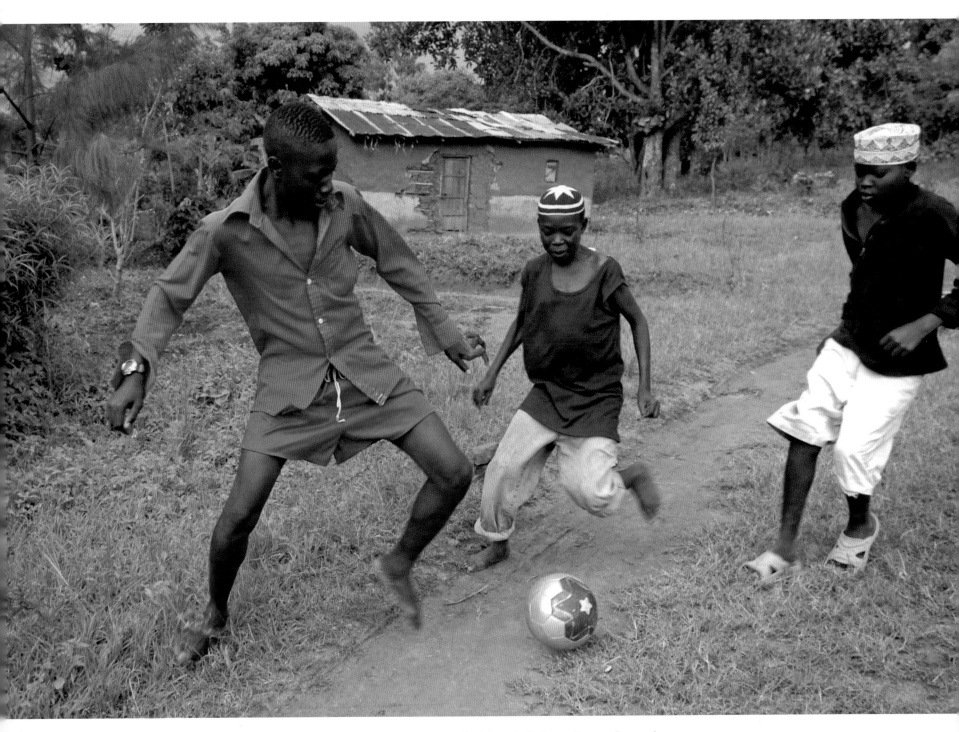

Children love to play games of pickup futbol anytime and anywhere

Large toy car made from bits of wire, old bicycle tubes, and discarded flip flops

One day, J.J. was watching his children and their friends. He saw how they played futbol together. How they made music together. How they built model cars together out of scraps of wire and old bicycle parts. They ran around laughing and talking and not caring about which religion anyone practices. They even joked about how the prayers and sermons in their places of worship were at times so long that some of the older people dozed off and snored loudly.

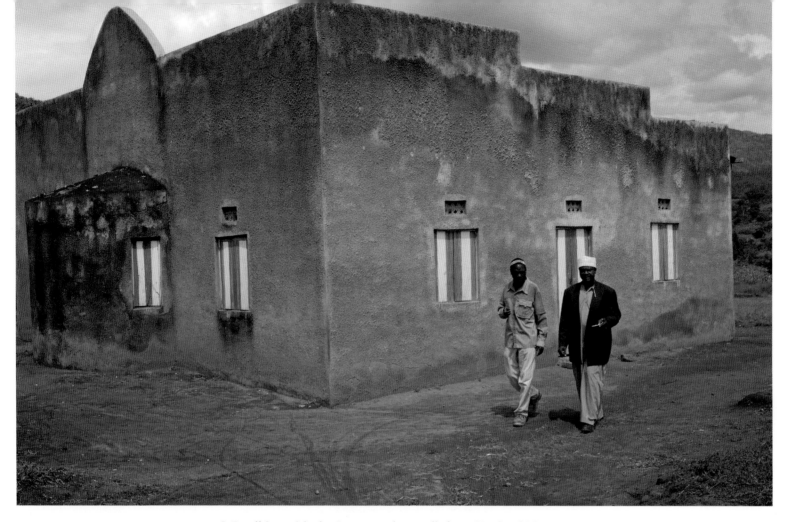

J. J. talking with the Imam as they walk from Nankusi Mosque

As J.J. looked at his children's friends, he realized they could all help him with an idea that he was working out in his mind. He asked the children to take him to their homes to meet their parents. He walked with them to their churches and mosques to meet some of his neighbors for the first time. The children had told their parents about the warm welcome and warm food they always found at J.J.'s home. The children had also told their parents that they sometimes did their homework with J.J.'s children. The parents were happy to greet the man whose family was showing such kindness to their children.

When he met with his neighbors, J.J. brought a message of cooperation and sharing. What was the one thing they all had in common? Coffee. His idea was that they form a cooperative for farming and selling their coffee. If they worked together they might get a better price and also spread a hopeful message. They would show the world that people of different religions can work and live together peacefully.

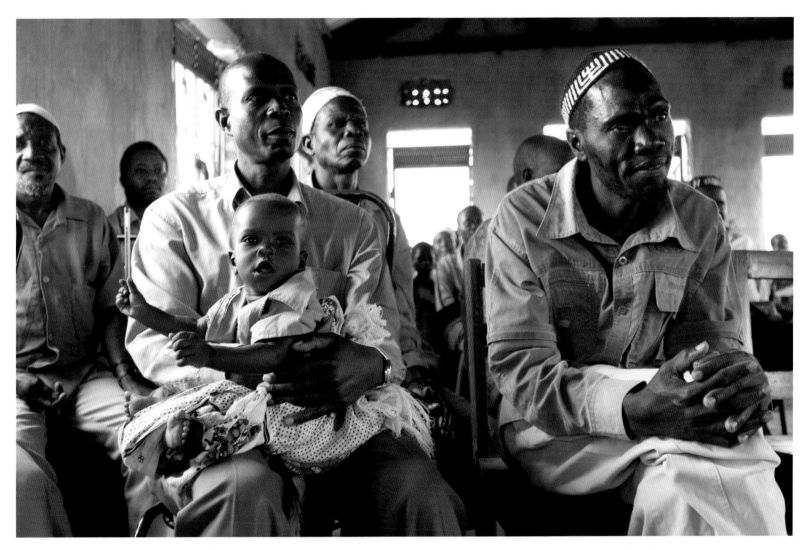

J.J. with farmers of Peace Kawomera coffee cooperative, inside Namanyonyi Anglican Church

At first J.J.'s neighbors were hesitant about joining the cooperative. They were used to staying in their own religious groups. But J.J. did not give up. He visited with his neighbors, trying to convince them to come together to grow coffee and spread peace. He continued to share his home and family with more of the neighboring children and they would often make music together. J.J. wrote a song called "In Uganda, Everyone Grows Coffee." When he walked the children home, they sang the song loudly.

Children learning the song "In Uganda, Everyone Grows Coffee"

Coffee cherries, the fruit of the Arabica coffee plant

As the children sang the song over and over, the words became a powerful message. In time, their parents began to trust J.J.'s idea. One by one, farmers joined together. In 2005, after the first growing season, there were 250 members of the Peace Kawomera Growers coffee cooperative. As of 2016, there were more than 1,000 farmers growing and selling their coffee collectively.

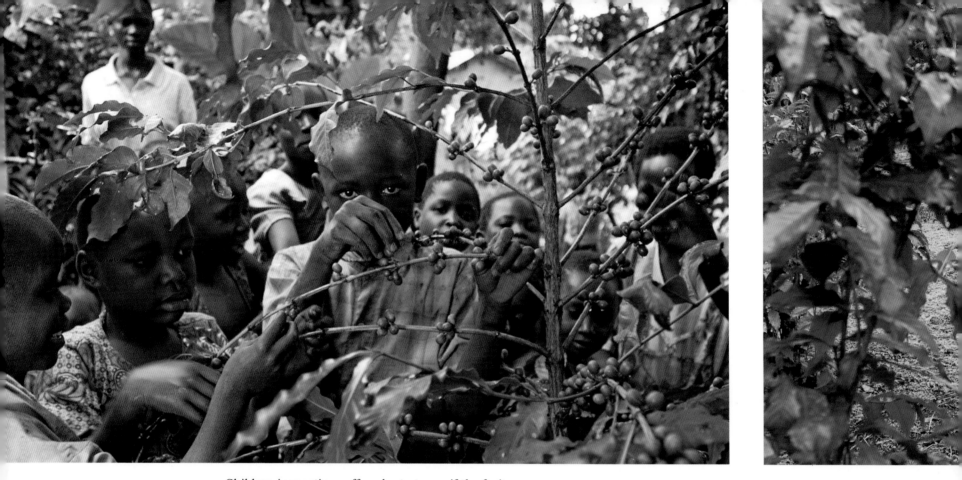

Children inspecting coffee plants to see if the fruit
is ready to be picked

Some of the best coffee in the world is grown in Uganda. Most farmers have small family gardens with just several dozen plants that they watch and prune constantly. The Arabica varieties of coffee grown in this region of Africa are delicate, and the ripe fruit has to be picked by hand, one piece at a time. The fruit, called coffee cherries, matures slowly; and the long branches of the plants bend low toward the ground as the fruit gets fatter. When the cherries are bright red, they are ready to be harvested. But the cherries don't all ripen at the same time, so it can take several weeks or even months of picking to bring in the entire crop.

Farmers make many trips to their fields to check the coffee plants and look for ripe fruit

At each garden, everyone in the family helps harvest the fruit, filling baskets cherry by cherry, a few pounds at a time. The children easily pick the low-hanging ripe fruit. Their small fingers are perfectly sized to squeeze between the unripe cherries and the shiny, ready-to-pick red ones.

Pulling down a branch to pick ripe coffee cherries

After picking, the ripe cherries are cleaned. Then the seeds, or beans, are removed and dried in the sun. When dry, the beans are shaken by hand to remove the outer skins. The raw coffee beans are then stuffed into large canvas sacks and carried to the cooperative office to be weighed. Finally the beans are sent to the port of Mombasa, in Kenya, and shipped to the United States, where they are roasted, packaged, and sold to consumers. Peace Kawomera has a contract to ship 40 tons (36.3 metric tons) of raw coffee beans to the United States each year. The cooperative also has Fair Trade certification, which means that the farmers are guaranteed a fair minimum price for their coffee as long as they follow Fair Trade environmental, labor, and trading principles.

Fresh, ripe coffee cherries, ready for cleaning

Spreading out coffee beans to dry in the hot sun

Shaking off the dried outer skins of the beans

Pouring raw coffee beans into a large canvas sack

Carrying sacks of coffee beans to the cooperative office to be weighed

Loading sacks of coffee beans onto a truck for the drive to Mombasa

Playing an embaire, a traditional wooden xylophone of Uganda

When the children are finished helping in the gardens, they gather in the yard behind J.J.'s home. Some of the boys drum out a beat on a wooden xylophone known as an *embaire*. The sound blares out in a rapid, upbeat tempo. The boys' hands move quickly, a full band playing on just one instrument. Nearby, boys and girls dance and sway. Their heads, hands, and bellies move to the left, while their hips, legs, and feet move to the right. The drumming and dancing go on and on. Soon the sunlight begins to disappear behind the western hills.

Dancing to the drumming beat of the embaire

J.J. comes out his back door clapping his hands to the beat and tells the children that they must be heading home soon to prepare for the weekend ahead.

"But J.J., we don't have school tomorrow, so we can stay out late tonight," one of the boys says as he hits the bouncing wooden slats of the embaire.

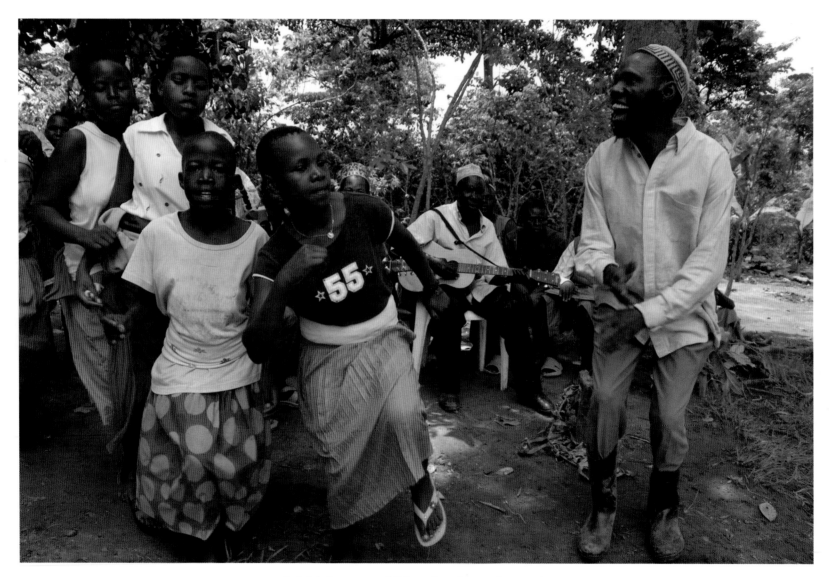

J.J. joining some children dancing to the music

Coffee plant loaded with green and a few ripe, red coffee cherries

J.J. smiles. He reminds the children that when they don't have school, people observe their days of worship. With Muslims, Jews, and Christians all living together and worshipping on different days, "maybe it is hard to keep track of them all," he says. Then J.J. pulls down a branch filled with green and red coffee cherries. He plucks the fattest and ripest red cherry and strips off the soft fruit. Holding the wet beans in his hand, he says, "Look here at our coffee. Inside each fruit are two beans. They don't like to live alone. We follow the example of coffee."

31

Although his idea was born in the aftermath of a terrorist event, J.J. has found a way to bring people together in Namanyonyi to work and live in peace. The coffee they grow is sweet, packed with flavor from the earth, but it is even sweeter because it carries the farmers' message of loving all neighbors.

J.J. sends the children home so they may bathe and get ready to have dinner with their families. The children laugh as they scurry away. The night turns dark, and a quiet hush falls over the village. For the next three days, the prayers of Muslims, Jews, and Christians will fill the air. Namanyonyi is one of the few places in the world where these sounds will be heard, each following the other in harmony.

SALAAM. SHALOM. PEACE.

Walking and playing music on the road that leads to Namanyonyi

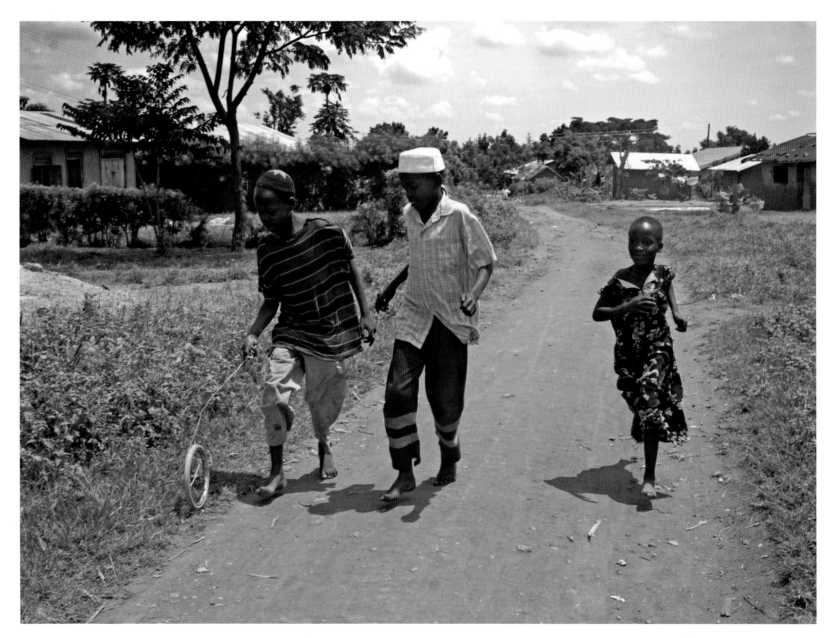

Children of three faiths playing together in Namanyonyi

Author's Note

Early in 2000, along the wildlife trail in Africa, I learned of an isolated group of practicing Jews: the Abayudaya of Uganda. I soon began a documentation project of this community, which led to my lengthy book *Abayudaya: The Jews of Uganda.* I met J. J. Keki, a Ugandan coffee farmer, while working on that book. As J.J. led me through his garden, I realized that although I loved to drink coffee, I did not know much about how it was grown or harvested. A few years later, when J.J. invited me back to Uganda to tell his story and take the photographs for this book, I learned all about coffee. But what impressed me even more was his community's story of religious harmony.

The village of Namanyonyi in eastern Uganda was like thousands of other rural communities in East Africa, where people of different religions stayed to themselves—until J.J. found a way to bring the villagers together through the formation of the coffee-growing cooperative. Namanyonyi is now a living example of religious cooperation.

Children and adults of three faiths—Judaism, Islam, and Christianity—live, play, and work together peacefully. Children embrace and respect religious differences, while their parents cooperate for economic fairness and improvement.

The formation of Peace Kawomera Growers cooperative in 2004 made a positive statement about religious tolerance as farmers of different religions joined together to market and export their coffee. They also became a Fair Trade certified cooperative. Fair trade is a business practice in which reasonable prices are paid and guaranteed for produce and products grown or created by people in disadvantaged areas of the world. Today many farmers of vanilla, cocoa, nuts, honey, cotton, and spices are also receiving fair prices for their crops as part of the fair trade movement.

At its core, this book tells a rare story of hope and religious harmony across generations. In this small corner of Africa, everyone is "growing" peace.

Richard Sobol

HOW TO HEAR THE MUSIC

Delicious Peace: Coffee, Music & Interfaith Harmony in Uganda is available through Smithsonian Folkways Recordings.

HOW TO FIND THE COFFEE

Delicious Peace coffee is available in the United States from the Thanksgiving Coffee Company.

GLOSSARY AND PRONUNCIATION GUIDE

Abayudaya (ah-bah-yoo-DAHY-ah): Jewish community of eastern Uganda

Arabica (ah-RAHB-ih-kah): finest quality of coffee; comes from the beans of the Arabica coffee plant

Christian (KRIS-chuhn): person who practices the religion of Christianity

Christianity (kris-chee-AN-uh-tee): religion of Christians, based on the life and teachings of Jesus Christ

church (cherch): Christian place of worship

civil war (SIV-el wor): war between different groups in the same country

coffee (KOF-ee *or* KAW-fee): drink made from the roasted and ground beans of coffee plants

cooperative (koh-OP-ruh-tiv *or* koh-OP-er-uh-tiv): business owned jointly by all the people who work in it

embaire (ehm-BUY-ray): wooden xylophone of Uganda

environmental (en-VIE-ruhn-MEN-tuhl): having to do with the natural world of land, sea, and air

Fair Trade (fare trade): worldwide movement that helps small-scale producers in economically disadvantaged areas receive fair prices for the goods they produce; certification means producers follow Fair Trade principles

Hebrew (HEE-broo): language spoken by Jewish people in Israel and other areas of the world

Imam (ih-MAHM): Muslim religious leader

Islam (iss-LAHM): religion of Muslims, based on the teachings of Allah (God) as revealed to the prophet Muhammad; Arabic word meaning "submission"

J. J. Keki (jay jay KEH-key): shortened name of Joab Jonadav Keki (JOE-ahb JOE-nah-dahy KEH-key), Ugandan musician, farmer, and founder of Peace Kawomera (Delicious Peace) Growers cooperative

Jew (joo): person who practices the religion of Judaism

Jewish (JOO-ish): having to do with Jews, their religion, or their culture

Judah (JOO-duh): ancient kingdom of the Biblical land of Canaan formed by two of the twelve tribes of Israel

Judaism (JOO-dee-iz-uhm *or* JOO-dey-iz-uhm): religion of Jews, based on the belief in one God and on ancient Hebrew Scriptures

Kampala (kam-PAH-luh): capital of Uganda

kawomera (kah-woo–MEH-rah): *delicious* in Luganda

Kenya (KEN-yuh *or* KEEN-yuh): country in East Africa

kippah (ki-PAH): head covering worn by Jewish men and boys

Luganda (loo-GAN–dah): major language of Uganda

Mbale (em-BAH-lay): city in eastern Uganda

missionary (MISH-uh-ner-ee): person sent into an area by a religious group to teach about the group's faith, or to do educational or health care work

Mombasa (mom-BAH-sah): city on the coast of Kenya

mosque (mosk): Muslim place of worship

Muslim (MUHZ-luhm *or* MUSS-lim): person who follows the religion of Islam

Nairobi (nahy-ROH-bee): capital of Kenya

Namanyonyi (nah-mun-YOH-nee): village in eastern Uganda, near the city of Mbale

Sabbath (SAH-buhth): day of the week set aside for rest and worship in some religions; observed by Jews from sundown Friday to sundown Saturday and by most Christians on Sunday

Semei Kakungulu (SEH-may kah-KOON-goo-loo): Ugandan tribal leader who founded the Abayudaya in the early 1900s

September 11 (sep-TEM-bur ih-LEV-uhn): date in 2001 on which the United States was attacked by terrorists who hijacked four airplanes that crashed into buildings in New York City and Washington, DC, and in a field in Pennsylvania

synagogue (SIN-a-gog): Jewish place of worship

terrorist (TER-ur-ist): person who uses violence and threats to frighten others

Torah (TOR-uh *or* TOH-ruh): scroll on which the first five books of the Bible are written; contains the body of Jewish sacred laws, teachings, writings, and traditions

Uganda (yoo-GAN-duh *or* oo-GAHN-duh): country in East Africa

World Trade Center Twin Towers (wurld trade SEN-tur twin TAU-urz): two very tall buildings that were part of New York City's World Trade Center from 1973 to 2001; destroyed by a terrorist attack on September 11, 2001

QUOTATION SOURCES

page 12: "Why should . . . our religions?" J. J. Keki. Interview with the author (Namanyonyi, Uganda, August 1–14, 2008).

page 30: "But J.J., . . . late tonight." Maccabee Keki. Interview with the author (Namanyonyi, Uganda, August 7, 2008).

page 31: "maybe it . . . them all." J. J. Keki. Interview with the author (Namanyonyi, Uganda, August 7, 2008). "Look here . . . of coffee." Ibid.

AUTHOR'S SOURCES

"Delicious Peace: Mbale, Uganda." Thanksgiving Coffee. http://www.thanksgivingcoffee.com/farmers/delicious-peace/.

Eyre, Banning. "Jewish Communities in Sub-Saharan Africa: Interview with Jeffrey Summit." Hip Deep. http://www.afropop.org/wp/10528/jeffrey-summit/.

Hasulube, Elisa. Secretary Manager, Peace Kawomera Growers cooperative. Conversation with the author, Mbale, Uganda, August 2008 and November 2009.

Kamulegeyeya, Siraji. Imam, Nankusi Mosque, Namanyonyi, Uganda. Conversation with the author, Namyanyoni, Uganda, November 2009.

Keki, Joab Jonadav. Founder of Peace Kawomera Growers cooperative. Conversation with the author, Namyanyoni, Uganda, August 2008 and November 2009.

Kolker, Jimmy J. Former United States Ambassador to Uganda. Conversation with the author, Brown University, Providence, RI, October 2008.

Mbiko Aisa Farmers Group. "In Uganda, Everyone Grows Coffee." Smithsonian Folkways. http://www.folkways.si.edu/mbiko-aisa-farmers-group/in-uganda-everyone-grows-coffee/world/music/track/smithsonian.

Moran, Ben Corey. Thanksgiving Coffee Company. Conversation with the author, Boston, MA, October 2008.

Namandosi, Sinina. Young people's representative, Peace Kawomera Growers cooperative board of directors. Conversation with the author, Nabugoya Hill, Uganda, August 2008.

Ngabirano, Henry. Managing Director, Uganda Coffee Development Authority. Conversation with the author, Kampala, Uganda, July 2008.

Ngugo, Samuel. Treasurer, Peace Kawomera Growers cooperative. Conversation with the author, Mbale, Uganda, November 2009.

Sizomu, Gershom. Rabbi and leader, Abayudaya community, Uganda, and brother of J. J. Keki. Conversation with the author, Nabugoya Hill, Uganda, August 2008.

Sobol, Richard. *Abayudaya: The Jews of Uganda*. New York: Abbeville Press, 2002.

Summit, Rabbi Jeffrey A. Ethnomusicologist; Research Professor, Department of Music and Executive

Director, Hillel Foundation, Tufts University. Conversation with the author, Kampala, Uganda, August 2008 and November 2009.

Various Artists. *Delicious Peace: Coffee, Music & Interfaith Harmony in Uganda*. Smithsonian Folkways. http://www.folkways.si.edu/delicious-peace-coffee-music-and-interfaith-harmony-in-uganda/world/album/smithsonian.

Yelusaniya, Ngugo. Leader, Namanyonyi Anglican Church, Uganda. Conversation with the author, Namanyonyi, Uganda, November 2009.

ADDITIONAL RESEARCH SOURCES

"History of Abayudaya." PVAO: Putti Village Assistance Organization. http://puttivillage.org/history-of-abayudaya/.

"Islam in Uganda: The Historicity." Muslim Population in the World. http://www.muslimpopulation.com/africa/Uganda/Islam%20in%20Uganda%20historicity.php.

Lidman, Melanie. "In Uganda, Coffee Co-op Blends Jewish, Muslim, and Christian Farmers." *Times of Israel*. November 17, 2014. http://www.timesofisrael.com/in-uganda-coffee-co-op-blends-jewish-muslim-and-christian-farmers/.

London, Charles. "Not Just a Cup, but a *Just* Cup." *O, The Oprah Magazine*. August 2008. http://www.oprah.com/omagazine/Coffee-Growers-In-Uganda-Promote-Peace.

"Museum Guide for Visitors with Children." 9/11 Memorial Museum. https://www.911memorial.org/sites/all/files/Museum%20Guide%20for%20Visitors%20With%20Children.pdf.

Primack, Karen. "Profile of a Leader: JJ Keki." Kulanu. 1999. http://www.kulanu.org/abayudaya/jjkeki.php.

Pyenson, Andrea. "Ugandan Beans Brew Taste, Tolerance." *Boston Globe*. June 3, 2014. https://www.bostonglobe.com/lifestyle/food-dining/2014/06/03/world-peace-and-good-music-through-coffee/fLYwrwNEuGyRividHIKbZI/story.html.

"Religious Symbols Meaning." Religious-Symbols.net. http://www.religious-symbols.net.

Rippo, J. A. "A Delicious Peace Comes from War Torn Uganda." *The Espresso*. May 16, 2012. http://www.theespresso.com/2012/05/a-delicious-peace-comes-from-war-torn-uganda/.

Schwartz, Penny. "Finding Harmony in African Folk Songs and Hebrew Prayers: Jewish Ugandans Blend their Voices and Cultures." *Boston Globe*. April 4, 2004.

Smith, Natalie. "What Happened on 9/11?" Scholastic News Online. http://www.scholastic.com/browse/article.jsp?id=3756477.

"Uganda." Jewish Virtual Library: http://www.jewishvirtuallibrary.org/jsource/vjw/Uganda.html.

"Where Coffee Grows." Coffee & Health. http://coffeeandhealth.org/all-about-coffee/where-coffee-grows/.

For Leonardo and Irmelin DiCaprio—working to make our planet
a healthier place and inspiring others to do the same.

Acknowledgments

My field travels in Uganda were undertaken together with Rabbi Jeffrey A. Summit, PhD, Research Professor, Department of Music and Executive Director, Hillel Foundation, Tufts University. His friendship and scholarship have been an important part of this work. I was also lucky to travel with Jonah Sobol, Russ Fill, John Servies, and Perry Granoff, who all lent their skills and insight to filming and recording the people and music of this community. This project was generously supported by the Lillian Goldman Charitable Trust, The Perry and Martin Granoff Foundation, Tufts University, Luminous Landscape Artist Project Grant, Smithsonian Folkways, Art and Betty Bardige, Robert and Sally Huebsher, Catherine Hayden, Larry Kopald, Leonardo DiCaprio, and Frank O. Gehry.

I also wish to thank Susan Cohen; Jeffrey A. Summit; Ronnie Mae Weiss; Louise E. May; Tracey Baptiste; Hena Kahn; Betty Bardige; Daniel Sobol; Laura Wetzler; Michael Schaffer; J. J. Keki; Rabbi Gershom Sizomu, member of Uganda Parliament; Moses Sebagabo, Kamanzi Anyello, and Buczana Willbroad at Uganda Runners Express; Harriet Bograd at Kulanu; Atesh Sonneborn at Smithsonian Folkways; Paul Katzeff at Thanksgiving Coffee; and Stephen Nemeth at Rhino Films for their support, direction, suggestions, and thoughtful critiques.

Copyright © 2016 by Richard Sobol

All rights reserved. No part of this book may be reproduced, transmitted, or stored in an information retrieval system in any form or by any means, electronic, mechanical, photocopying, recording, or otherwise, without written permission from the publisher. LEE & LOW BOOKS INC., 95 Madison Avenue, New York, NY 10016, leeandlow.com

Map on page 2 created by Paul Colin, Cezanne Studio
Photograph on page 8 of Semei Kakungulu is in the public domain
Book design by Paul Colin, Cezanne Studio
Book production by The Kids at Our House
The text is set in Bookman Old Style
Manufactured in China by RR Donnelley
(HC) 10 9 8 7 6 5 4 3 2
PB) 10 9 8 7 6 5 4 3 2 1
First Edition

MIX
Paper from
responsible sources
FSC
www.fsc.org   FSC® C144853

Library of Congress Cataloging-in-Publication Data
Names: Sobol, Richard, author, photographer.
Title: Growing peace : a story of farming, music, and religious harmony / Richard Sobol.
Description: First edition. | New York : Lee & Low Books, [2016] | Includes bibliographical references.
Identifiers: LCCN 2016004452 | ISBN 9781600604508 (hardcover) ISBN 9781643796499 (paperback) eISBN 9781620143551 (EBK)
Subjects: LCSH: Agriculture, Cooperative—Uganda—Juvenile literature. | Coffee—Uganda—Juvenile literature. | Fair trade foods—Uganda—Juvenile literature. | Religious tolerance—Uganda—Juvenile literature.
Classification: LCC HD1491.U45 S63 2016 | DDC 334/.683373096761—dc23
LC record available at http://lccn.loc.gov/2016004452